WALKING WITH LIGHT

Walking With Light

WRITTEN BY ELIZABETH THOMPSON

Edited by Katherine Arnold

Elizabeth Thompson

Contents

Dedication — vi

I. Missing — 1

II. Struggling — 15

III. Loving — 29

IV. Falling — 37

V. Growing — 69

VI. Changing — 83

VII. Walking — 93

About The Author — 108

Thank you to Katie, without whose help these poems would never have seen the light of day.

And Jason, who inspires me daily and walks in light by my side. You saved me before I knew how to save myself. I love you.

I. Missing

The Sleepwalker

his eyes are bleary
lids heavy from the weight of his world
closed to his own misery
he's only sleepwalking

he'll never run
his ankles and feet can't move
from the weight of the shackles
of what they always told him

"for your own good"
to pay the bills
settle into a life
that's no more than sleepwalking
as ivy creeps upon the stones,
built up around his dreams
that he'll only ever see because
he's sleepwalking

the white noise of his life
music and laughter fade to static
and the only rhythms in his bones
are his deadened directionless footsteps

through a haze of the bodies
no love in his empty relationships
bubbles of isolation trapped in their own blur
passing by and never connecting

a plastic bottle life
beats a rhythm not quite right
living in aluminum cages

never seeing organic life
the nerves no longer crackle
with sweet electric fire
the soul no longer hungers
it aches, but not for more

a world filled with sleepwalkers
and I'm so painfully awake
in this dark, but crystal-clear nighttime:

I hope there's someone else awake.

Sleeping

The earth sleeps
While we sleepwalk through it
She creaks
under our dead, lifeless feet
Brown and grey circles on her winter ground

But I am a restless one
Awakened, awakening, I need to move
Darting through the trees
The world at my heels
Cars, dust, concrete:
dogging me to a crawl

We began in the earth with our fellows:
Creatures, animals, beasts
Now on feet — we tread on them beneath.
we don't see
that In standing we've fallen so far

Far from purpose — from intent — from the real
We cover the flaws, we cover the pain
But my skin and bruises are raw — and I am unashamed.

I'm only woman, but I'll fly, and I'll rise
Sing the phoenix's song, I take to the sky
And with my words and my song
And I'll stir this cold world that's
Been sleeping too long.

Anywhere, USA

Anywhere, USA, is that it?
Up for anything — the same lame old shit
Anywhere is where they want me to be
Anywhere, anything isn't good enough for me

The problem is the "any": you simply don't care
The problem is "any" stretches through the air
When "any" fuels all and "any" is fine
And you live without purpose —
and I can't find mine

So many content not to answer their call
Spending their nights watching screens on the wall
So many won't jump, afraid that they'll fall
So they go with the crowd — doing anything at all.

Anything you can do just to fill up the void
Recalling old dreams now just leaves you annoyed
The "any" takes the place of the visions you no longer see
Because hurting is something that you don't want them to see

So you hide all the hurt behind boozing and smiles
And money and cars and all the latest styles
Your feet aimlessly tread 1,000,000,000 miles
'Til you're in anywhere anyhow.

I'll move and I'll fight to be where I want to be
I'll move and I'll work no matter who stares at me
I will live my life and I
Will push back against the sea
Of anything that dares to keep me
From all that I know that I can be

This apathy's old and it's time to put it away
To rise up and claim every single new day
To renew your vision and to now dare to say
I've had it with Anywhere, Anything, USA

How the World Works

I have a lot of ideas
About how the world works
How it could work
And how it should work
Imagining my own utopia

Wanderlust

I remember where
the red fern grows
I saw it
once upon a time
I climbed rock faces and dipped my toes
in wild rivers sublime

I remember because my wanderlust
stretches her borrowed wings
and the cracks in my wild
mother nature's soul
aches for some long-forgotten thing

that my eyes have never seen
Spirit aches to roam
eyes, feet, hands, legs, and back
body cramped from lack of motion

each twinge along its ridges
reminds me I should be on a mountain range
each deep sore throb of muscle
tells me I'm made for more.

Empty

I am ravenous.

Starved for love, for life, for it all.

As a child, I could not speak
Could not tell the truth for fear

Of consequence.

Children are resilient.

I held

The wounds, the pain

Until one day

They came out

Writ on my body

The words I could not speak.

I needed the pain to be seen

To be real

To heal

Nostalgia

My thumb lingers
Over the profile picture
Of an old friend.
Do I click? Do I dare?
Curiosity killed the cat.

"Photos of us."

Buffering.

In a millisecond
I am catapulted
Through the barrage of images
Each flick of my finger
A step further back
Through a life I forgot existed
Through a time I can't quite recall

How grounded in my present
That I have forgotten
A life.
I can't have lived this many years.

I blinked and they were gone.

It's like watching old films
Black and white movie reels
Of emotions
Processed real-time, sped up 10x

The footage watched in fast-backward:

Trauma
Heartbreak
Love
Curiosity
Joy
Companionship

Things that took weeks, months,
years to recover from
Launched through my soul
At the speed of scroll

No wonder
When I look back in time
I am so drained.

Perhaps memories
Are best digested
In morsels.
Savored.

Photo books
Should come with a warning label:

"Only consume at real-time speed."
My heart is too delicate
To recall it all
at once.

II.Struggling

From The Front Porch

From our front porches
The world seems so open and so wide
This platform may be little
But at least I'm not inside

From here I smell the open air
And from here I feel the breeze
From here I hear love's whispered tones
Float to me from far-off seas

My arms in whorls of wood may rest
On front gates
And latticed fences
But the steps that lead out to the road
Are what I fight against

A girl on a bike rolls down the path
Her smile rings through the air
Her wheels make lasting divets in the ground
Though she's gone from here, and off to there.

I know each leaf that hangs from the oaks
Their patterns memorized
Precious little in this street
Does not attract my eye

This porch has known a hundred feet
Supported a hundred shoes
And under her weathered, dusty slats
Lost knick-knacks show us clues

Of souls which fell in love outside
The old bright red front door
Of salesmen tromping 'round the town
And collectors for the poor

In the dirt, a hundred lives are led
Humans; multiplied by score,
About their tasks, they move about
That's all they ask, no more

Know more is what I'd like to do,
I'd like to move and go
To feel that dirt road on my feet,
to work and live and grow

I've seen so much and felt so much
I know a million things
I'll never move, but the view is great,
When you're on a front porch swing.

Churn

Push
Pull
Torque
Turn
Move
Jump
Scream
Turn
Roll

Spinning like a turbine
the ones that will change the world
pointing to the sky generating
the winds of change
I will never stop speaking
never stop moving

they say it's a new calendar
a new year
it's just another number
another notch in Time's belt
as he holds his scepter
Change
menacingly over the heads of those who dare
to defy him

I fear him not
I know that when I make my peace
with Time
then Change
is my friend

For I work with change
I move to create it
to change for good

for energy
for power
for love
for peace
for the world

for myself
I refuse to be anything less than a titan
ranked with the greats.

Pace: *Ode to a Team*

We set the pace
we set it to hell and back
and we set it together

and the blood, the tears, the screams, the groans
that's our music
and it's loud and it's hard and it's real and
we push

we push past the limits of human capability to be more
to do more
to grow more
to learn more to never stop

To fight our enemies
to fight our demons
to fight the things that keep us from achieving
all that we could ever be

and we can be it together because
together is more
and when I look in the eyes of my team at the end of
the day
no matter what
this is my team

this is dignity and honor and love
and trust
trust to know that you are only there to make me better
and I will do what I can to make you better

because when the blood dries and the sweat clears
and we walk into the cold night
the rain washes away the pain
and I am reborn. and I have been reborn.
And that is our victory.

Cardiac Arrest

Thump. Thump. Thump
My steady heart beats a rhythm of 60 per min
My legs pound the pavement, calves, ankles and shins
All's well in my ribcage then the attacks begin

1.2.3.
A rhythm — like clockwork I'm steady, on beat
The pulse of my red blood won't stand for defeat
A stalwart and strong set of hands and of feet

Then thunk, thump, thunk thunk, irregular
First one skip, then two
as blood, as cardiac muscle increases its pace
Like runner's adrenals before the big race
The rhythm accelerates as I first see that face and...

Then STOP.
Rhythm's gone.
Beats don't drum.
This rest wasn't written in my music,

No blood.
No brain.
No reason.
Swimming vision.

Cold hands
Looking at yours
So strong
Intertwine and warm mine

My vision darkens slowly
Where did my steadiness go
As my once stable body quavers
Those eyes are the last thing I see

And your heartbeat is the last thing mine wants
As it fails
In cardiac arrest.

It's just a dream
Those eyes they stare
A drink of water
A refreshing change

From those I know
The life I live
The fight I face
But there's nothing you give

But just a dream
I close my eyes
Feel electric touch
Always re-realizing
It's just a dream

Memories

Palm trees turning, swaying in the breeze
I hold the past in my palms
But I already blew it into the wind

It's scattered, perhaps close to you.

Beneath my shut lids, the images play
Maybe they're on your cutting room floor.
Do you ever sift through them, that far in the past
Or is it something that you can ignore?

My foolish scatterbrained heart found it
More important
To live my life — something better, I thought
Chasing pipe dreams I aimed for,
ignoring the good
Forgetting the joy that was there.

I dream now of palm trees, of shy giggly laughs
I dream of warm nights, humid days
I want to wake up and to see
That sweet stare
But alas, the coffee's only decaf.

Turning

Watch as empires rise and fall
Leaving scorch marks on the earth

Watch fathers leave their sons and teach
Hard-heartedness from birth

Watch mothers hold their children
Sobbing reaching anywhere for care

Watch daughters try to change
The world with little left to share

All the world is turning, turning
Spinning round in space

Turning so fast humanity's eyes can't see the pace

Turning like a top and hurtling on its path in space

Turning, turning, hoping, praying for a bit of grace.

Fitting In

Have you ever been told
That you don't fit in
Somewhere?

Again and again?
That you won't fit in ...
anywhere.

Your voice
Your thoughts
Your body
Your heart

So many times until

It seems
You don't even fit
Your own skin?

So, you're dying to shrink?
Dying to live small?

My darling, you deserve space.
Take it.

Body dysmorphia

Puppet

I'm not a marionette
Held up on a string
At beck and call
Tied up
For you
Time to cut the cord.

Panic

It builds
Increasing
Crawling up from my insides
Sticking in my throat
Its icy hot fingers strangling my vocal cords
Terrified
To cry for help
To show weakness
Need
I can get it under control...
Badasses don't have panic attacks.

It sticks in a lump at my neck, filling my insides
I can't breathe.
Gasping for air, gulping:
A silent killer.

Every inch on fire
An explosion of energy with no hold to cling to
Yet an internal combustion
Like a dying star
Turns out, badasses do need help.

III.Loving

The Greatest Adventure

The greatest adventure for me
Is to live on this earth with you
Each minute, each hour, each day
Is filled with an ocean of blue

A hug in the morning, a kiss in the night,
Your body beside me when I turn out the light
Your calls in the daytime, your voice in my ear
Your presence enough to combat any fears

At home or abroad, by mountain or sea
(though home is when you are with me)
We'll cherish the familiar, embrace all the new
As long as I live in each instant with you

Your love is my strength, my comfort, my light
Together our lives make our hearts take new flight
To new goals and new visions,
no matter how grand
We can conquer them all
when we're joined by the hand

Each tiny surprise is the world's greatest gift
Learning about you just makes my heart lift
Discovering our love is life's greatest treasure
Bringing joy and brings peace that can never be measured

Each new step we take is a breathtaking climb
Round each corner a new year

with discoveries to find
A host of new challenges, friendship and growth
And together we master them, quickly or slow

My adventurous spirit can finally rest,
Knowing each day and night I discover the best
Of life's greatest gifts, and so many it's true:
That life's greatest adventure is always loving you

Jason

Sometimes it is impossible, during the course of events, to know that history is in the making.

Other times it is easy.

With you, I knew that earth shattering was happening.

Knew that the potential

was there for something great.

How could I have known just how great?
How, even now, can I know just how great we will be? How much this love will grow?
To outrank foolish couples of lore,
Romeo and Juliet, Paris and Helen, Troilus and Cressida?

We are no fools, we are titans, and no one has ever loved anyone the way that I love you, and no one ever could.

I know because when I look at you
and I feel my love for you,
I know that nobody but I could ever feel a love this intense.
And a love like this could only ever be felt for someone like you.

Listening, Watching, Feeling

The way you always wear the same socks
The way everything seems just a little bit better
when you're here.
The fact that I'm more inspired to write than I've been
in months and
the annoying fact that all
the good stuff I write lately is about you
because my writing comes from
my strongest emotions.

And the strongest good ones now seem to stem from
you.

And I'm so scared.

By how beautiful you are.

By the way your eyes look when you kiss me.
By the way I always feel whole
when you're around
but I know that just like me
your mood has the capability to turn on a dime
but I don't mind
because I'd take you any way you came

As long as you did.

And when I come to you —
And the road opens up to open highway it feels
like my life is opening up before me and that's
why I am speeding down the road at breakneck
speed on a crash course and
I'm so happy it's like

my insides are out and in and I'm terrified
to crash and wrap myself around a telephone pole
a wreck of wires, tires, twisted metal, burns, smoke,
burned out tired flesh and scars.

I'm a wreck.
I'm a wreck that was righting itself
mending.

I didn't need you.
I didn't expect you.
And I still don't need you to be whole.

But I want you.
Because somehow when you run your hands
over me my twisted metal doesn't feel so

mangled.
but the way the sun catches
the cracks in my paint
are like stained glass refracting the new light that you bring.

so that I give it back to the world
double what I ever dreamed

And I'm giving it back here
and now
with my words.

All you ever need to do
is give me the chance
for listening, watching —
and feeling

IV.Falling

About Him

This is about him
This is about him because clichés
are dripping from my lips, from my heart like
ink onto the paper
from my bleeding soul — through my veins coursing
through
every inch of me guided by
the electric pulse of his lips
on. mine.

This is about him because just the thought of him
stretches the corners of my mouth into a version of my
10-gigawatt smile into
15 hundred megawatts
I didn't even know it had.

And it powers my heart, conducting the rhythm
of beats

1234
2341
3421
4321

This is about him because dear lord those
kisses could last forever in eternity
and there's nothing PG about when these titans collide

like ancients like gods
and there's truth to our myth and no fairytales
only raw, R-rated real life

And there is nothing PG about you and me
because you see the records in my head are
turned off for once in my life the rat race of
never enough is on pause and when the needle
scratches
and we're done —

the circuit blows.
And *still* there's light.

and that tender hold he has on me is in his
arms and I feel
I can move mountains
and if not I'll just climb them
but now I don't have to trek alone because
that's what we two were made for.

To take on this world, to rock boats,
to make it happen

to storm the trenches of apathy and discontent
with the steel toe boots of sweat and blood
and the high of achieving everything you want and
hopes and prayers you don't even dare to put words to.

But now I know I can. Because...

this is about him. Because what I gave up
believing in long ago exists and is real and
in front of me

tangible, touchable, tastable.

I'm in love with plants.

and they're beautiful and complex and their
vines and flowers and leaves remind me of
limbs and elbows and knees —
and it's so appropriate because he's so and we're
so beautiful

and I'm tangled in a storm of worrying about
me but now worrying about we
and I'm intertwined with this man and entangled in
emotions that are unprecedented and because of that
my judgement can't judge

and all I know is that it's beautiful, wonderful, magical,
terrifying strange up and down and
completely perfect for me and not puppy love

not naivete because no he's not my first but he damn well
might be my last and now he knows and
when our lips touch I can't breathe and I don't need to.

So this is about him.
and it's intense and it's raw,
and it's writing my heart.
Some people use three words and
they use them too lightly and too soon
but all I'm saying is —
that this —
this is about him.

Melt

In the day time
You are my first hello in the morning
And my soul awakens when you answer
Bringing me awake to who and what I am
My frozen heart dares to thaw
To you and you alone

You are the rock I cling to
Though I shouldn't, couldn't admit I need you
I need you.

I need to hold
My missing piece
My soul
In another body
When yours joins with mine, through hearts or hands
It's then that I am filled

When we are together in presence
It seems that no one else is needed
A void is there when you are gone
A hole where my other piece is

You fit so snug inside my heart
I'm so fully me with you

Eight months and still I grow
To know you more
With a lifetime to learn
To become ourselves together

I wax and wane poetic
I write fictions
Poetry
Exposes the truth
For reality is true in our dreaming

I lie in this bed without you
Yet I feel the echo of your arms
It's a comfort and reminder
Of a shield against the demons

At night when you are holding me
In the garden of your arms
The night is not so fearful
As our breathing becomes one

I pretend that I am stronger
Than the fears which plague the heart
But with you, I am laid bare
My strength is a different kind

In the truest of reflections, I
Admit my fear, a different kind
A bigger and a stronger sort
Which requires the strength of a greater kind

I'm only strong because I must
Be so, or else collapse
But now that I've found my soulmate I
Know that someone else is by my side

Only you know my deepest fear
Know the passions that I hold
Yet at this time our journey has
Only begun to unfold

I want to see the world with you
Each crack within this land
Every ivy every sky and
Every path through every wood

Our entrapment in institution
Though it's only for a time
Weighs heavy on my bird like heart
That longs so much to fly

So I fly right now to you, love
While we wait to soar on high
I prepare right now for what's to come
For together we'll rule the sky

Jazzman

Jazzman, jazzman, jazzman
Has played music on my heart
The sweetest song to sing along,
Even when we are apart

The jazzman plays my song of love
Sets my heart to counterpoint
There's something sweet, to know he's mine
The hottest player in the joint

Strumming on my heartstrings
Don't know how he knows the tune
Each sharp and flat he navigates
This man lifts my every gloom

He hears beauty in my dissonance
And gently changes key
From minor chance into major love
My sweet man plays for me

Loving a Lion

It is not easy, loving a lion
It is worth it
But this love takes a lioness

a lion is a challenge
He would not, does not settle
Yet — because of this I know
the love is real:
investment

In his roar — there lies
emotion
expected
and unexpected

They vary as
each day he surveys
his path, and his self
A discerning soul

He roars of dreams
he roars of fears
he cries out on the lonely path
one he *used to* walk alone

The lioness alone can hear
can truly understand
an instinct more powerful than survival
draws her to him

Their paths, drawn and made
for one another
for no other speaks their tongue
no other dares to roar

Deaf to odds
deaf to doubters
I will walk with you
as we are a pride of our own

I will hold you in your doubts —
when your roar is but a whimper
I will listen and love your heart
for it calls and speaks to mine

I will laugh from my soul
with joy with you

I'll share your dreams
I'll share your strife
I'll share each day
If you let me share your life

Born to roar
created to strive
created to need to drive
My love, my soul, my heart.

Untitled

I never dreamed about forever
Cause my life's just too messed up
But the moment that your lips touched mine
I had no time to duck

Always moving round in circles
Always chasing my own tail
And every time I'd try to pause
My mind has just been too frail

You pulled me out of bed one day
Then into bed one night
You've been my dawn, you've been my dusk
You're a faintly flickering light

A light you have that I can see
The others give you grief
I see your childlike, kind true soul
And all that lies within

Beneath the ranting and complaints
Of a guy that's just fed up
Is a man who'd never hurt a fly
Who'd rather give a hug

I don't know what else I can do
I don't know what to say
But embrace those tender loving arms
And let you in my heart to stay

So when I talk about the future
It's no joke as you might guess
I've got dreams of you in white and black
And me in a long white dress

Leo Season

Into the world he came
Into my life he came
A fiery ball of love and potential
On this spinning rock hurtling through space
Fate on a barreling path to meet me

The day the earth was blessed
With the greatest soul I know.

Born of the sun
Of light and power
Smiling and laughing into my every hour.

Leo. My lion. My king.

Endless energy that burns
Its stamp sealed onto my heart
Pummeling down every door
Bright eyed, an endless roar

Yet tender, protective, and true
Fierceness threads its way
Through everything you tackle
Each thing you discern to do

A wise lion
Full of courage to delve
Into life's greatest mysteries
To dine with me at a feast
Of intellectual delight

He holds my heart
Tenderly in his strong hands
He has the power to crush with just a word
Yet chooses to nurture and grow

Grow our love each day as he
Vowed he would
The day that he vowed "I do"
And yet everyday on this journey we take
We vow, "I do, I do, I do."

I love you with action for that is our way
As lions we prowl through this life
Surveying the kingdom, improving the den,
And making this house our home.

We dream of cubs together
Others to give our love
A family to cuddle, laugh
And a joy to hold and hug.

Nuzzles and love ferocious
Big dreams stretch far and wide
It's Leo season, darling,
and I'll roar by your side.

Just After Dark

Just after dark
There's a glow
That comes on
Not outside
But in my home

The lights flicker on
Warm
Illuminating
All that lies within

The smells
Of a warm meal
Diffuse through the halls
Wafting up and down the stairs

My ears are tickled with
Little voices
Of students
Whose fingers brush lightly
Or bang irreverently
On keys or strings

And your voice
Warms my heart
With patience
That I could never muster

Not even with myself
Yet you
Fill our hearth
And my soul
With the glow
That is
Our love.

Asleep on the Couch

Comfort
It is all we seek
Having known strife
Having known
Loneliness
The deepest well
A burning ache

Electric points of contact
Comfort
Is anything but comfortable
It is the electric
Touch
Of skin on skin
With the intoxicating scent
Of familiarity that wakes each fiber of the nose

As we settle
Bodies melding together
And into the softness
Of the cotton pillows
The silk of your skin
Underneath the slightest gritty brush
Of stubble

Your eyelashes flutter
Across your cheek
Casting a long shadow
Onto my soul
Night after night

Your head slowly drops
The sinew in your neck
In slow motion
Ripples a release of tension

As you slowly
Fade onto my lap
As we love
And fall
Asleep on the couch

100 Little Moments

100 little moments
A roar in the silence that was once my life
A hug in the morning to remind me my worth
A silly dance in the garage in the morning
A giggle in the bedroom
Making the goofiest jokes with my best friend
Dreaming for the future
Together.

Holding hands through the struggle
Wrapped up in you
Tears when it's too much to bear
A soul that sees your beauty when you can't
100 little moments

The flash of the sun on your glasses
Blue as the eyes they protect
Blue as the car with the windows rolled down
As the wind flies through my fingers like
100 little moments I want to hold onto
That have made up this year

Our very first Christmas morning
Waking up in the bed next to you
Santa came and filled each stocking
Stuffed like our little home to the top
Brimming over with cheer

A home filled with laughter and friendship
The "firsts" of boundless memories to come

A place where we gather with loved ones
Where all are welcomed with warmth and hugs

New traditions we're making
Library dates, reading nights
Music on the TV
Learning to waltz — though I'm not sure I taught it right!

Exploring the town together
Strolling the park in the warmth of the sun
Farms, farmers markets, and sunsets
Giant houses (one day we'll have one!)

Driving to go get ice cream
On boiling hot summer nights
Cuddling your arm on the way there
Glances stolen while you drive
Nuzzling your shoulder
Love sweeter than any treat

Cuddling all the way through quarantine
When we both get to work from home
Lunch dates staring in your eyes
I hope this feeling never goes

Celebrating milestones
With friends and family and ourselves
Cherishing each moment
As we all build our lives

100 little moments we'll build
Kids, our business, and love and care
Each year will bring so many more and I can't wait —
As our family and lives, we share.

Teach Me To Love

Teach me to love like mother nature
Her hands hold the earth steady and true
While the world flows smoothly through the seasons
My love, I'll always give my best to you

I'm no poet but I'll study lover's ways
Of Shakespeare, Cummings, Whitman, and Van Gogh
They praise the riches of nature in its glory
But my love's beauty outshines the full moon's brightest glow

Teach me to love like brothers teach their sisters
Lead me to protect my love and have no fear
Give me bravery to stand tall in all life's struggles
And hold love close when enemies draw near

Show me beauty in the stillness and the silence
To be the eye in every hurricane and storm
A light when darkest night surrounds you
I'll shine on you and keep you safe and warm

Sunflower, turn your face skyward to meet me
I'll be your sun and shine on you each day
Like nature's eternity we will forever
Love one another until we're old and gray

At end of day I know I am no master
That's why I look to you my love to teach
Hand in hand we'll learn love and life together
Forever, now that true love, we have reached

Teach me to love through cycles of the seasons
Warmth in winter's cold and summer's sun
Though breezes of the world may swirl around us
Together we're united, we are one.

The Squishy Parts

I want to love your squishy parts
Vulnerable, and kind
Authentic, brave, and honest
The deepest corners of your mind

I want to hold your softness
To squeeze until it spills
Into my arms and heart where I'll
Protect you from life's ills

I promise to love all of you
Each crack and scar I'll kiss
My lashes brush across your cheeks
With softness, joy, and bliss

The world may turn, not understand
The beauty of each part
Your deep blue eyes hold all the keys
To unlock your whole heart

Your squishy parts are beautiful
Like all the rest of you
I'll take eternity to love them
And show my squishy parts to you.

Islands

We were islands once,
my love
Floating
Adrift on a sea
Raging around us
Life crashed on our shores

No green, friendly shore
Visible
From our land

Formed by fire
Fed by need
Our peaks reaching ever higher
We were islands once
My love

Until the ocean brought my shore to yours
And the sands of the beaches fit
The reefs, a perfect puzzle piece

Green and blue, a perfect tapestry
Ever adding more

We were islands once my love
No more, no more, no more.

Pillow Mate

Rest with me, come rest with me
Be my pillow mate
Warm me through the coldest night
Mold you to my shape

Cover me in you, my heart
Rest your head right here
With you, the journey through the night
Holds no reason for fear

Hold me in your arms so tight
As the night moves into day
The clock says go go go, get up
Yet here, is where I stay

With your blue eyes across the bed
When I open mine each day
The bluest sky I'll ever need
Is in your love, every day

New Eyes

Mine open slow
Calmed by the weight
Of your body by mine
A calming, warming gravity
Of your presence

An energy
Strong, gravitational
A calming pull
Stay.

Bleary, blurred, tightrope
Walking, toeing
The line between sleep and wake

Where reality is now dream
The golden hour
Of the heart

A puzzle piece
I fit
I fit like our bodies
Designed to snug into place
Like the fabric of our lives
Sewn together with threads of dreaming

New eyes meet yours
Yet half-asleep
Could I be dreaming
Magnetic. Hypnotic. Pulled.

Peace. I find again
With new eyes. Here.

V.Growing

Blessed

When moments come
And waves crash on your face
Tears will always dry
In the sweet warm embrace

Of those whose love
Always keeps you whole
take it all in
For you're a blessed soul

Be open to love
Be vulnerable
For only by giving love
Will we ever know

Without our human flaws
There'd be no need for love
No need for hope
Which reigns above

Without money, or walls
Or jewels in a chest
Wrapped in the arms of love
You are always blessed.

Light

Light is eternally
E
P
H
E
M
E
R
A
L

Sliding through
The air
Casting its shadow
On all that it touches

I see it

Changing everything

Omnipresent

Then

Gone

How to capture
With words
To paint the unpaintable
Uncapturable

Diffuse.
Glow.
Flicker.
Cast.
Beam.
Rise.
Shadow.
Glint.
Glare.
Glimmer.
Fade.
Vanish.

Shattered

Can you hear it?
The ceiling —
it's shattering.
Sparkling shards of glass
litter the ground.
Those below
must watch their step
while the privileged few ascend.
Only to find another barrier
which we could not see
from below.

When the ceiling shatters and the glass
dazzles with rainbows of color

it is only an illusion.
We must watch our feet
or fixate on the glass.
We cannot gaze beyond to see
what is possible.
Let us not shatter the ceiling.
Let us dismantle the barriers themselves
and throw a ladder down
to raise each sister up.

———

My vow: I will not stand on the shoulders of those still
oppressed.
To do so would dishonor our foremothers.

Autumn Sunset

The sunshine
She calls
When she breaks through
From beneath the blanket of fog and rain
In mid-October

And so I go
I run.
I run for no other reason
Than
To feel
To experience
Her rays stroking
My skin

To fly through an autumn sunset
To breathe her cold air
That stings each follicle
Each inch of my lungs
To remember
How it feels to be alive

She kisses everything faintly with orange

The woods still tangled in moss
From the river, just now receding
A mustiness in the air
One can see the origins of Halloween
In the cast of the amber dying light

I run
Trying to catch
The dying light
The last of the rays of the sun
And to embrace
The coming sleep

Of the change
In seasons
As the world turns
The light
Does not leave
It merely transforms.

Unfolding

I am a story untold,
to unfold
Under the loving pages of caring words

A word can change the world
If we only listen

To the melodies of the story + songs of those
Who are there in the story
On the following page
And all we've got to do is turn

Turn to face the eyes of a friend
For that is where their story's told
Being written in their steps, their hearts,
their souls
And all we have to do is read it.

But most hate reading, they tell me so
And I can't quite find why.
Perhaps their story has become so big
They don't have the time to try

But there's danger in only one story
When yours is all there is
When all you know is what you know
You can't see the beauty in his

Story, and it's sitting in front of you
If you'd just stop and see
The lines + characters may be different,
But there are so many common themes:

"Like love and truth and peace and joy
Like anger, lust and fear
Each glad and bitter human tale
Unravels, inscribed here

The web of tales is thick and rich
Its threads ensconce us all
Just tug at one small part and see
One language, known by all. "

Mud on My Boots

Mud on my boots is the mud on my soul
No sweeter balm will I ever find
Cooling the fire of my thirst for the unfettered life
Freedom in the dirt, where I'm from

Home base
Is where the wild things are
The stains on my clothes and my feet are the map
Of the places I've been
And the road to the places I'll go

The cracks in my hands trace energy lines
To the hands of companions
Our fingers intertwined makes the power of change
Stronger than we ever could be alone

The Springtime Makes My Soul Pop Up

The springtime makes my soul pop up
It likes to peek outside
It feels the change that's in the air
It's ready to feel alive

The springtime makes my soul wake up
My eyelids feel the sun
As green comes back and fights the dark
My soul's dance has begun

The spring brings barefoot strolls by day
and star-led walks by night
and Time goes back to cloistered sleep
as Spring begins her flight

For three months my soul moves with her
Engaged in ecstatic dance
They laugh and smile and love and fly
For when Winter comes — they can't.

Sacred Spaces

Will I be seeing you?
In all the sacred spaces?
All the hamlets of light that remain?

They were once all considered sacred
They still are (sacred, though not considered so)

Will I find your footprints
On the path right outside your front door?
Is your spine accustomed to leaning
Against the raspy bark of your white birch tree?
Does a swing hang for your daughter
From its branches
So she can meet the sacred?

Or will their memory vanish with you?
Will you wander the wilds of uncut wilderness
Or shall I find you at the palm-lined shelter of a cocktail bar
Sipping a drink named for a place
You'll never see?

We cannot love what we do not know

We cannot know what we cannot see

So go find your sacred places
Then seek to show the world
Why they are worth saving.

"Eco"

Being a good steward

Of our home

Should not be a personality trait, a hobby, or an interest. It should not be interesting

at all.

Being stewards

should be so programmed into society

into our ways of life from the highest levels
that to discuss it
is as boring
as chatting
about
the
weather.

VI. Changing

The Feast

The world looks like
An ice cream cone
And I want to lick it dry
To catch the dribbling melting bits
So sweet you want to cry

And lap up life like a begging pup
Its sweetness on my tongue
I'm ravenous for life's banquet
For more desserts to come

I'm at Adventure's table
While Destiny sweeps the floor
And Lady Danger courts my taste buds
While Experience guards the door

So bring the second helping
I'll devour it course by course
And you'd better learn to clean your plate
Lest I try to feast on yours

Simplicity

Simplicity

Strips away excess
It allows

The truest
Most pure form

Of the incandescent beauty of things

To take its place in the starring role.

With the trappings and trimmings gone

The truest, simplest, nature of things

Will dazzle your deepest soul.

My Words

These words trip over my tongue
Like feet on cracked roads
Syllables on its tip stick in my throat
These lips, my instrument
These words, my notes.

Fleeting

To bottle emotion
To make you feel
To snatch a will-o-the wisp out of the air
And place it
Into a jar

Only to find
That upon examination
It loses its mystery
Its grandeur
Its beauty.

Catch-as-catch-can.

Poems Aren't "Written"

A wise poet
once said
That poems aren't
Written

They just
Happen.
And we poor poets
Are just
The sad, hapless oils
Who are tuned
Just right
To these moments
Of ecstatic wonder

So time after useless time
I see them
Sparks flying
In the tedious, glorious, everyday

Trying pathetically to
Verbalize
Everyday magic

To thrust the unseen
Heartbreakingly stunning
Moments

That most people
Barely notice

Poets are
Desperate souls
Thrusting moments
Under our readers' noses

Yawping

"Here, look!"
but, like perfect rainbows
They are lost
The moment we try to define

The electricity-filled, crackling-with-energy,
brush of your lover's cheek
The flickering of a candle
The inside-warming sensation
Of a favorite cup of tea

Try to view your life
Just for a moment
As your own personal collection
Of poems

Until then,
I am
The poor sucker
Who is just
Trying to
Help
You see.

Passion

I write
For passion
I write for the peace of my soul
Some days, like any of those called to craft
slippery squirmy words into sentences
Like a child grabbing bubbles from the air,
grasping at a phrase that's only
there for a tiny moment
I would fall to my knees for the right words
To describe the shining ecstasy of life
brought to me
By the beauty of the world I tread:
Passing through

Some days I find them, those words.
They are the only gift I have.
My passion project.
My "pay it forward" for being given a pair of
eyes
And a tender heart
Softer than the touch of my loved one's skin
on mine
And a mind
Only sharp enough, alas, to form and see the words

Sometimes.

But I write.
Sometimes it takes an instant.

Sometimes an eternity,
while kaleidoscopic chords of a favorite song
Tugging at my loose heartstrings.

Since I was born this strange child
It is the least I can do
To try
To paint the world
As I see it
And pass on the gift.

So I write.

VII. Walking

Truth Teller

My lips are on fire
From an ignited soul
My voice is cracking
From the truths I know

Legacy

Goddamn this fucking bullshit.
Do I have your attention?
Stop shitting on me.
Fuck this godforsaken capitalist garbage.

I'm at the end of my rope.
Time for you to notice.
Notice your mother.
Notice this place from whence you
Crawled out of the sludge
The dust, the purest of clean waters —
Before you too aim with your waste
And turned those waters into toilets,
Then distilled it into the liquor you sell
To bored children
So they're too docile and confused
To understand their impending doom.

They're waking up.
Waking up to see the rape of the dusty cracked
soul, crying with thirst
Violated
Day after day after day by fracking sledgehammers.
As the ground coughs forth gas,
Mixed with the dust and poison.
Blackening the sky and the lungs
of the children of earth.
A bitter price to pay for a drink of oil,
A high of money and power.

Drink up.
Drown yourself
So the drink in your veins
Replaces your red blood,
Too heavy to move
Fat on the flesh of the bespoiled future.

We will rise.
We will rise from the sewage
Of a land spoiled by chemicals
And we will till the soil anew.
We will heal the land with new farms, new respect.
The hands of the man will provide
Enough for each need.

The liars and imposters,
The talking heads
Will topple
From the seat of power
To be trampled by the dirt-starved feet
Of a generation awake
Who demand satisfaction
For the burning of this house.

We will rebuild this home.
We are prepared for war.
We pray for peace.
We will accept one, for the other.
Be ready, for change is in the wind.
What force will you fight for?

The Vessel

Never forget
that you are a soul
inhabiting a body
that your essence
your highest self
is only living temporarily in this earthly form

This vessel
is your dwelling
it withstands all the earthly trials
of this harsh, relentless world

Buffeted by the storms of life
Traumas
are imprinted in your aching muscles
wrenching at your wearied bones
etched into the worry lines
on your beaten brow.

So be kind.
Walk soft.
You are more than this skin,
This tissue, this shape.

And yet.

Your beautiful soul;
your essence of love

Deserves
nothing less

than a home,
cared for.
Respected
by its tenant

The world will be cruel enough,
Gorgeous soul;
give your vessel
the same love and light
which touches all corners
of each space you enter

Wrap your body
in respect and care
until you can muster love.

Evolution

Don't shrink to fit the box
The world provides
Make your own.

You were designed
To shed your skin
100 times
To grow
To grow again...

It stings.
It strains.
It cracks.
I promise each new evolution is more
unimaginably
breathtaking
Than the last.

They've never seen the likes of you.
It's about time they did.
<u>Self- actualize.</u>

Call to Love

The world will try to break
Your soul

It will rip and tear
It will chill the crevices
Bone deep

Into the cracks of
Your shattered skin
Slash your veins
And drink you dry until
You can't imagine
Any softness left

Don't let it.
The world will try
To make you hard
To shape you
Into its essence
Mold you
Into a lifeless soldier
Of cruelty
Mocking others
To draw them in
To the same fate.

Don't let it.

The world will sneak
Try to disguise its lies
Decorated in gold
And filtered Instagram veneers
Manicured lawns and plants
Ripped from their motherland
Covering lies and landfills
Clawed remains of a savage waste
Empty promises of a dying capital
Bereft of meaning.

My darling, don't you DARE let it.
You are a warrior of light.
A child of love
Claimed for love at birth
Softness and goodness
Aren't weakness
They are your unbreakable
Unshakeable
Undeniable strength.

The world needs you
To change
To transform it
Back
To what it should be
What it could be
What it will be.

Child of the sun
Lion with mane of light
Roar into the darkness
And breathe hope into the cracks

Let the wildflowers of your
Heretical words
Spring forth and blanket the land

So the souls of the others
Can be called home
To grow life anew.

One Last Gasp

Sometimes
After good reigns
And your heart is light

Evil, when it comes
Inevitably feels darker

And for all your valiant striving
At the end of evil's time
With its dying screams
Its last gasps
Are hardest to bear as it desperately
Exerts its power
One. Last. Time.

Let the life and death of evil
Remind you
Never to be complacent again

Lest we lose the glimmer
Of a new dawn
We so bravely sought to see.

Though our arms are tired
From trying to lasso the sun back
From her slumber

Let these years have been a reminder
To never fall silent again.

Death

I did die that night —
The night of my own reconciliation.

I died to the idea that I would ever
give up
again.

I died to the feeling
of worthlessness
of emptiness

I died to weakness, to fear, to the past.

I am the most beautifully molded diamond
Unbreakable
Yet cut with 1,000 unique fractals

Made for light.
That night, I died to darkness.
I remembered
that I walk with light.

Walking with Light

Walk with light.
Softly, gently
Feeling each blade of grass sweep across the soles of
your feet
Allow your toes to sink deep
Into the mud-lined riverbeds
Breathe in deep the same air
That circulated on this globe for millennia

You share the life force of billions.

Tread softly
For billions more have yet to come
Leave minimal traces
Yet let the traces you leave
Be so brilliant
That your light reaches
Every crack, corner and crevice of dark.

Let each footprint
Be a place
Where light begins
And ripples out
To illuminate all who need it.

Let your light touch the immaterial things
The ones that will be remembered
In song
In dance
In poetry

Live your life
Like art
Like poetry
Like song.

Walk with light
With the quiet dignity of the trees
Bow to none
Yet accept no deference
We are all citizens on light
Born to tread with grace
To embrace love
One another
And beauty.

We are the soul of the world.
Let us walk with light.

About the Author

About the Author

Beth Thompson lives in the Chicago suburbs with her husband, Jason. She has been writing since grade school and always dreamed she'd actually get the chance to put her words into the hands of the world.

In her free time, Beth loves to practice yoga, spend time outdoors, and read voraciously. She's currently in the process of pursuing her MBA in social impact. Her dream always has been and still is to change the world in a positive way.

I hope these words make you feel something, and help you walk through this world with light.

This book contains a few poems with underlying themes pertaining to mental health struggles. Please see the below hotlines if you are struggling, and remember you are never alone. Sometimes it is the most beautiful souls who struggle the most.

National Suicide Prevention Lifeline: 800-273-8255

National Eating Disorders Helpline: (800) 931-2237

www.ingramcontent.com/pod-product-compliance
Lightning Source LLC
Chambersburg PA
CBHW072013290426
44109CB00018B/2228